The Forgotten Art of Making Old-Fashioned
Jellies, Jams, Preserves, Conserves, Marmalades, Butters, Honeys and Leathers

Illustrated by Margo Letourneau

Designed by Carl F. Kirkpatrick

Clarissa M. Silitch, Editor

Published MCMLXXVII by

YANKEE, Inc.

Dublin, New Hampshire 03444

This Book Has Been Prepared by the Staff of Yankee, Inc.

First Edition

Copyright 1977, by Yankee, Inc.

Printed in the United States of America

All Rights Reserved

Third Printing 1979

Library of Congress Catalog Card No. 77-83101

ISBN 0-911658-80-7

Contents

Foreword

One day last summer, when I had splurged on a roast of beef for a family occasion, I thought I'd like to make a spicy (say barberry or parsley) jelly to serve with it. Leafing through my considerable store of cookbooks, I found, alas, that unless I fell back on plain grape, or apple jelly, the beef was to stand alone.

You never realize something is missing until you start looking for it. And that is the reason for this cookbook. I was struck by the fact that in none of the many cookbooks I searched were there more than a few recipes for jams, jellies and that ilk, all lumped together usually in one chapter with other preserved foods like pickles, relishes, or sauerkraut — which practice doesn't leave much room *for* more than a few of each. And I wondered why there *wasn't* a book that told you how to make *all kinds* of jellies, marmalades, jams and, of course, conserve, that rich sweet country-farmhouse treat.

Thinking it over, I remembered that *Yankee* occasionally published old-time jelly and preserve receipts and resolved to look through its recipe file. Well — not only did I find meat jellies aplenty — barberry, parsley, horseradish, mountain ash, mint, and more — but a whole treasure trove of all the rest, including, as this book does, fruit butters, honeys and leathers. Spreads made of every imaginable fruit — and nuts and vegetables too! Among the rarer — chestnut jam, ripe (also green) tomato preserve, venison jelly, clover honey, paradise jelly, pumpkin conserve, sweet green pepper jelly and apple marmalade. Not to mention old favorites made of strawberries, blackberries, peaches, apricots, oranges, lemons, plums, blueberries, apples, quinces, pineapple and whatever. All sent in over the last forty years by readers of *Yankee* Magazine and *The Old Farmer's Almanac*. More than enough to make a book, and another book too (of pickles, relishes and *that* ilk).

So here's the book; we hope it fills in that gap in *your* cookbook shelf; it certainly has in mine!

Clarissa M. Silitch, Editor

canning jar

1 Jellies

Perhaps the prettiest preserve of them all is homemade jelly — there is nothing like a row of clear translucent, stained-glass color to warm a housewife's heart and enrich the family table. Definition: fruit juice and sugar cooked until the mixture will hold its shape when taken from glass or jar, but is easily spread or cut with a spoon.

Why does homemade jelly taste better? Two reasons. One — the ratio of fruit juice to sugar is much higher than with commercial jellies (by law at least 45% fruit and 55% sugar, whereas with most homemade products the ratio is more like 60% fruit juice to 40% sugar); two — many delicious jellies simply are not commercially available.

On Jelly Making

The secret of jelly making, of course, is to make the stuff JELL. Like most other cooking processes, understanding is the key. Jelly is made up of fruit, acid, pectin and sugar. The **fruit** is washed and cut up, but not, except for pineapples, pared, and not, except for quinces, cored; peels and cores contain a lot of the pectin. Berries and other small fruits are crushed rather than cut up. Thus prepared, the fruit is put into a large open cooking kettle of stainless steel or enamel. Water is added only in the amount needed to prevent scorching. With many crushed soft fruits and berries, there will be enough juice so that no added liquid is needed. Cover, bring to boil and cook until the fruit is soft and the juice is flowing (berries will need only a couple of minutes' boiling, hard fruits like apples 15-30 minutes).

Suspend a jelly bag (or cheesecloth and colander) over a large bowl, and pour the contents of the kettle into the bag. (See page 12.) Let the juice drip through the bag into the bowl overnight for best — clearest — results. If you squeeze the bag to extract the juice faster, you will get perfectly good juice, but it will be cloudy, and so will the jelly made from it.

Acid thickens, **pectin** jells the juice when it is cooked.

With some fruits, the extracted juice will contain all the acid and pectin required for jelly without supplement. These fruits are: *tart* apples and blackberries, crab apples, green barberries and gooseberries, currants, cranberries, grapefruit, eastern grapes, lemons and plums. Acid or pectin must be added to other fruit jelly. Sweet apples and quinces are high in pectin but low in acid (add vinegar or lemon juice to the extracted juice). Apricots, blueberries,

colander

cherries, figs, peaches, pears, pineapples, raspberries, rhubarb, strawberries, and all overripe fruit are low in pectin content. Additional pectin or tart apple juice must be added to the juices of these fruits to make them jell properly.

Sugar, the fourth important component, increases the volume of the juice, sweetens it, sets the gel, makes the jelly tender (rather than leathery) and helps prevent mold and fermentation. Corn syrup or honey may be substituted for up to one-quarter the amount of sugar required in a jelly recipe. Jellies made without added pectin (apple jelly, for example) require less sugar per cup of juice, but longer cooking to reach the jellying point. The longer cooking time, however, does have the advantage of evaporating any excess water in the fruit juice.

THE JELLYING POINT. So, the trick is — to have just the right proportions of acid, pectin and sugar, properly prepared juice, *and* to cook the mixture to just the right stage. When you do not use commercial pectin, the jelly stage is reached when the temperature of the mixture is 8°F above boiling. The boiling point of water varies with the altitude, being approximately 212°F at 1,000 feet or less. To find the boiling point in your own kitchen, use a candy thermometer to determine the actual temperature at which water breaks into a boil. Add 8 degrees to this and you will have the temperature at which jelly will be ready to jell in your kitchen. Depending on the altitude, this will be 220°F or more.

Lacking a candy thermometer, you can ascertain the readiness to jell by either the metal spoon test or the refrigerator test. Begin testing about 5 minutes after you add the sugar. Take a spoonful of juice from the kettle, cool a minute, holding the spoon at least a foot above the kettle, then tip the spoon so that the juice runs back into the kettle. If the liquid runs together at the edge and "sheets" off the spoon, the jelly is ready. Or put a saucer of juice in the freezing compartment of your refrigerator for a couple of minutes. If the mixture firms up in this time, the jelly is ready to pour into jars.

ADDED PECTINS. A word about added pectins. Jelly can be made from low-pectin fruits by combining the low-pectin juice with apple juice, half and half, and using 2/3 cup of sugar for each cup of the combined juices. If the low-pectin fruit is blueberries or strawberries, add 1 tablespoon lemon juice for every 2 cups of the jelly juice.

You can extract your own fruit pectin from oranges. First, peel the fruit, removing both orange and white layers. Separate the white part from the orange part of the peel. This thick white lining is the pectin source. Reserving the fruit and orange peel for other uses, chop up the white part in a food mill. Mix each cup of chopped-up white with the juice of one lemon and let stand for one hour. Then add 2 cups of water, heat to the boiling point and boil for 5 minutes. Remove from heat and leave this mixture standing overnight. Next morning, reheat to boiling point and boil for 10 minutes. Strain through a jelly bag (see page 12) into a bowl, pour into hot, sterilized jars, and seal.

To use in jelly making, bring equal proportions of juice and sugar (1 cup sugar to every cup of juice) to a full rolling boil, then add half as much orange pectin as you have juice (1/2 cup pectin to each cup of juice) and boil the mixture to the jellying point.

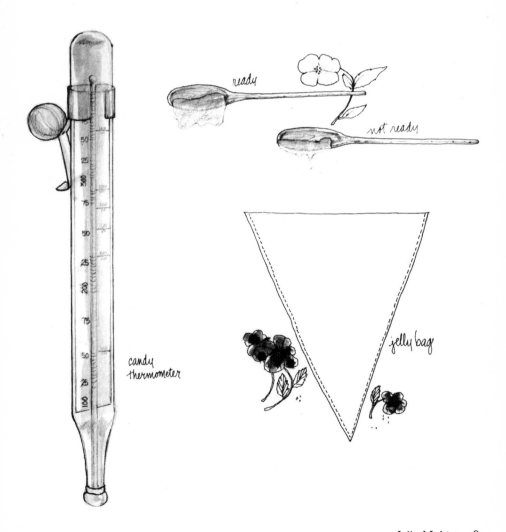

ready

not ready

candy thermometer

jelly bag

Commercial pectins are available in both powdered and liquid form. MCP is a common brand of powdered pectin, Certo of liquid pectin. Some people prefer the powdered as having fewer added preservatives; others prefer the liquid, which has been on the market longer. For best results with whichever type or brand, note the manufacturer's own directions.

Generally speaking, however, if a recipe specifies *powdered,* use powdered; if the recipe calls for *liquid* pectin, use liquid pectin. For one thing, powdered pectin is added to the juice *before* it is heated and *before* the sugar is added. Add pectin to the juice, heat this mixture to a rolling boil, then add the sugar, bring back to a full rolling boil and boil for one minute. Then pour and seal. With liquid pectin, the juice and sugar together are first brought to the full rolling boil, the mixture being stirred constantly while it is heating to the boil. Then add the liquid pectin and after reestablishing the full rolling boil, keep the mixture at the boil for 1 minute. Then pour and seal.

POURING AND SEALING. Wash and sterilize your glasses (and caps, if you use them) by heating in a kettle of cold water that is gradually brought to the boiling point. Turn off the heat and leave the glasses in the kettle until ready to use. (Jars should still be hot when you pour in the jelly.) Then drain the glasses and set out on a level surface. Skim the foam off the jelly, taking care not to stir it in. Ladle the jelly *as soon as it is ready* into the glasses, holding ladle close to the glass as you pour to help eliminate air bubbles, and being careful not to let any jelly dribble onto the rim at the top of the glass. Leave 1/8 inch headroom with modern screw-band tops or 1/2 inch headroom when using paraffin to seal the jars. If you *do* slop jelly, wipe the rim clean before sealing. When the jelly is in the glasses, put a teaspoon in the middle of the jelly and stir it around once to eliminate air bubbles. Then seal.

If you use screw-band tops without paraffin, put on the cap and screw band tightly. Invert the glass for a second, then turn right side up. The jar will form a vacuum seal as the jelly cools.

If you use paraffin, have it ready and melted. It is safer to melt paraffin like baking chocolate — in a double boiler, but if you watch it carefully, you can melt it over direct heat. You want it just melted, *not* smoky. (If you don't watch paraffin carefully while it is melting, you can end up with a bad stove fire.)

Pour a thin layer of melted paraffin over the jelly, taking the glass in your hand and tilting it slightly so that the paraffin flows to every part of the rim to ensure a perfect seal. Prick any air bubbles that appear in the wax. As the wax cools, these bubbles can turn into holes right through the paraffin layer, and thus through the seal. When the wax is cool, and firm, cover each glass with a metal top or a circle of paper or foil held on with a rubber band or masking tape. Label each glass and store in a cool dark place.

One final note — do not double the recipes that follow — the jelly will either not jell or not be as good. Make two or more separate batches instead.

Apple Jellies

Besides the basic apple or crab apple jellies, a whole raft of different jellies may be made with apple juice, by using spices and herbs, or by combining the juice with an equal amount of the juice extracted from another fruit (or fruits); the apple juice provides natural pectin, the second fruit provides natural flavor.

BASIC APPLE or CRAB APPLE JELLY

tart (underripe) apples or crab apples
water
3/4 cup sugar for every cup of juice

Porters or MacIntosh will make a sweet jelly; Gravensteins or Greenings will make a spicier jelly.

You will need enough apples to fill a large kettle. Wipe the apples and remove the stems and the blossom ends and cut in quarters (do not pare — a large amount of the natural pectin is lodged in and just under the skin). Cut crab apples in halves. Put prepared apples in a large stainless steel or enameled kettle. Add cold water to almost cover the fruit — there should be about an inch of apples out of the water, but you should be able to see the water level in the kettle. Cover and cook slowly over low heat until the apples are soft.

Mash the fruit slightly while it is still in the kettle. Suspend over a large bowl a damp jelly bag or colander lined with wet cheesecloth. (You can run up a flannel or muslin jelly bag on your sewing machine in minutes — see drawing.) The juice will drip through the bag or colander into the bowl. Pour the kettle contents, fruit and liquid, into the bag or colander and allow the juice to drip through into the bowl overnight. Meanwhile, do something else so that you will not be tempted to squeeze the bag to hurry things along. Squeezing (or pushing through the colander) will not hurt the flavor of the jelly, but it *will* cloud it as minute particles of pulp will come through into the juice.

When the juice has dripped through, measure out 4 cups (leave the rest for another batch). Heat the sugar in a double boiler; with 4 cups of juice, you'll need 3 cups of sugar. Bring the juice to a full rolling boil, then add the heated sugar and bring the mixture back to a full rolling boil. Boil *quickly,* stirring, until the candy thermometer reads 8 degrees above the boiling point (see page 8) or until the jelly sheets off the spoon (see page 9). Skim and pour into jelly glasses and seal (see page 10).

SPICY APPLE JELLY

Follow the same procedure for Basic Apple Jelly *except* that when you put the apples into the kettle to make the jelly juice, you also put in 4-5 whole cloves and a 2-inch stick of cinnamon bark before you add the water. Then continue as in Basic Apple Jelly. (You can remove the cinnamon and cloves from the kettle before you put the fruit into the jelly bag.)

GINGER APPLE JELLY

Cut 1/2 peck tart apples in quarters, leaving skin and cores. Add 2-3 pieces crystallized ginger and water until you can just see the water level. Cook until soft and drain through a jelly bag. Add as much sugar as juice and let boil until the syrup sheets from the spoon. Just before taking off, stir in the strained juice of one lemon. Skim and turn into glasses. This will make 8 tumblers.

SPICED CRAB APPLE JELLY

5 lbs. crab apples
2 cups vinegar
1/2 teaspoon powdered mace or
  allspice

2 cups water
1 tablespoon whole cloves
2-inch piece of cinnamon bark

Prepare apples as specified in Basic Apple Jelly. Tie the spices in a bag and cook with the apples in the water/vinegar mixture until the apples are soft. Finish as for Basic Apple Jelly.

ROSE GERANIUM APPLE JELLY

Make Basic Apple Jelly, but before pouring the jelly into the glasses, put a sprig, or a couple of leaves of rose geranium in the bottom of each jar. A distinctive flavor. You either love it or hate it. Try this with other herbs as well — basil, marjoram or thyme, for example. Add green coloring if desired.

APPLE MINT JELLY

Either put leaves of fresh mint in bottom of jar before pouring in apple jelly or proceed as follows.

1/2 cup tightly packed mint leaves
    and stems or 1/4 cup dried mint
1/2 cup boiling water

Steep the mint in the water until the mixture has cooled. Strain out the mint and add the liquid to tart apple juice in a ratio of 1/2 cup mint extract to 4 cups apple juice, plus green coloring to suit. Proceed as for Basic Apple Jelly.

Combination Apple Jellies

These are made exactly like Basic Apple Jelly, using the proportions of sugar, apple juice and second fruit juice given below. As always, make jelly in batches of only 4-5 cups of juice at a time.

BARBERRY-APPLE JELLY

Three parts apple juice to one part barberry; 3/4 cup sugar per cup of combined juice. Pick the berries before the first frost, while some are still green.

BLUEBERRY-APPLE JELLY

Use equal proportions of apple and blueberry juice, and 1-1/8 cups of sugar to each cup of the combined juice. Add 1 tablespoon of lemon juice for every 2 cups of the fruit juice.

CRANBERRY-APPLE JELLY

Equal parts cranberry and apple juice; 3/4 cup sugar per cup of combined juice.

CHERRY-APPLE JELLY

For every 1-1/2 cups apple juice, use 1/2 cup cherry juice. Sugar: 1-1/16 cups to each cup of the combined juice.

RASPBERRY-APPLE JELLY

Use equal amounts of apple and raspberry juice and 3/4 cup of sugar to each cup of combined juice. Add 1 tablespoon lemon juice for every 2 cups of fruit juice.

RHUBARB-APPLE JELLY

Equal parts rhubarb and apple juice; 1 cup of sugar per cup of combined juice.

STRAWBERRY-APPLE JELLY

Equal parts strawberry and apple juice; 3/4 cup sugar per cup of combined juice.

PARADISE JELLY

12 cooking apples   6 quinces
1 lb. cranberries   1 cup sugar per cup of jelly juice

Quarter the apples and core the quinces (do not peel), discarding stems and blossom ends. Wash and pick over the cranberries. Put the fruit in a large kettle with water barely to cover and boil until soft. Strain through a jelly bag. Then boil the juice, with 1 cup sugar for each of juice until the jellying stage (see page 8). Pour into glasses and cover with melted paraffin. Makes 12-14 glasses.

Other Old-Fashioned Jellies

blueberry

AUTUMN JELLY

6 ripe tomatoes
6 medium cooking apples

2 lbs. underripe blue grapes
1/2 cup water

Wash the fruits. Slice the tomatoes, slice the apples and mash the grapes. Combine and cook over moderate heat for 15 minutes. Strain through a jelly bag. Add 1 cup sugar for every cup juice. Boil rapidly until syrup coats the spoon. Turn into hot, sterile jars. Seal with paraffin.

BEACH PLUM JELLY

Pick your beach plums in late August or September. You don't want them too ripe — half should be underripe for higher pectin content. Place the fruit in a kettle and add just enough water to prevent scorching. Simmer gently until the stones separate from the fruit. Pour the fruit and juice into a jelly bag and let the juice drip overnight.

I. Without Added Pectin

Measure out 4 cups of juice and bring to a rolling boil. Boil for about 10 minutes, then stir in 4 cups of sugar and boil rapidly until the jellying point (see page 8) is reached. Skim the jelly and pour into glasses. Seal with paraffin.

II. With Added Pectin

Measure 3-1/2 cups juice into the kettle and add 6 cups sugar. Bring this mixture to a boil, stirring constantly. Stir in 1/2 bottle of liquid pectin and bring again to a boil. Boil hard for 60 seconds, then skim the jelly, pour into glasses and seal.

BLACKBERRY JELLY

Prepare the blackberry juice, and then cook as directed in BASIC APPLE JELLY (page 12), using 3/4 cup sugar for every cup of juice.

BLUEBERRY JELLY

4 cups juice (takes about 2-1/2 qts. whole berries)
7-1/2 cups sugar

1 tablespoon lemon juice*
1 bottle liquid pectin

Stir sugar and juices thoroughly, bring to a boil over high heat (add a dab of butter to reduce foaming), stirring constantly. Add the pectin, boil hard for 1 minute, remove from heat, skim off any foam, pour quickly and seal or cover with hot paraffin at once.

*To dwarf or bog blueberries, add 1/4 cup lemon juice.

CHOKECHERRY (WILD CHERRY) JELLY

Pick about 3 quarts bright red (not ripe) chokecherries or underripe wild cherries. Stem and wash. Add water just to cover and simmer until the fruit is soft. Put fruit and juice into the jelly bag and let drip. Then, put 3 cups of the juice into the kettle with 6-1/2 cups sugar. Bring to a high boil, stirring constantly. Add 1 bottle of liquid pectin and bring back to a full boil. Boil hard for 1 minute, stirring, then remove from the heat. Stir and skim. Add 1/4 teaspoon almond extract, if you like. Pour into glasses and seal.

CORNCOB JELLY

Remove the kernels from 12 ears of red field corn. Boil the cobs in water just to cover for 30 minutes. Remove the cobs and let the liquid drip through the jelly bag. In a kettle, mix 3 cups of the cob juice with 1 package powdered pectin. Bring to a high boil and then stir in 4 cups sugar. Boil hard for 1 minute, then remove from the heat. Stir and skim, adding a little food coloring if you wish, then pour into glasses and seal.

CRANBERRY JELLY

1 quart cranberries
2 cups water

2 cups sugar

Simmer cranberries in the water for 20 minutes or until soft. Rub through a sieve (or put through a food mill). Add sugar and return to the stove. Bring to a rolling boil and cook for about 5 minutes. Pour into a wet mold or glasses immediately as jelly hardens quickly. Chill.

SPICED CRANBERRY JELLY

Prepare as Cranberry Jelly, but put 2 sticks of cinnamon, 2 cloves and 1/4 teaspoon salt into the pot before you cook the cranberries.

CURRANT JELLY

Gather currants (cherry currants are the best for jelly) the last few days of June, or the first few days of July. An excellent color is obtained by using equal amounts of white and red currants. Pick over and wash the fruit, but do not stem. You can add water or not, as you prefer. Without water, mash the bottom layer of currants and put the rest of the currants in whole. With water, add 1/4 as much water as you have currants. Cook slowly until the fruit is soft and white. Strain and drip the juice through a jelly bag.

To cook jelly, measure out 4 cups of juice and bring it to a full rolling boil for 5 minutes. Add 4 cups of heated sugar (heat sugar by placing in a heavy frying pan in the oven at low heat, stirring the sugar occasionally), boil the mixture 3 minutes, skim, and pour into glasses.

wild grape

GRAPE JELLY

Wild grapes or underripe Concord grapes make the best jelly. Wash and stem the grapes. Put into the kettle, mash down and cook slowly for about 10 minutes, until the juice flows freely. Water may be added a little at a time if necessary to prevent scorching or sticking. Strain through a jelly bag and leave the strained juice overnight in the refrigerator to allow the white crystals that sometimes form to settle. In the morning, pour off the juice carefully, discarding the sediment, if any, at the bottom.

Measure the juice, and proceed as for Basic Apple Jelly (see page 12), using 3/4 cup sugar for every cup of juice.

Two kinds of SPICED GRAPE JELLY are:

Venison Jelly

3 lbs. fully ripe grapes
1/2 cup apple vinegar

1 teaspoon cloves
2 teaspoons cinnamon

Wash and stem the grapes, place in a kettle and crush thoroughly. Add the vinegar, cloves and cinnamon. Bring to a boil, cover, and simmer for 10 minutes. Place the fruit in a jelly bag and strain out the juice. Measure the juice and complete as follows

4 cups juice
7 cups sugar
1/2 bottle liquid pectin

Place the juice and sugar in a large saucepan and blend. Bring to a boil and at once add the bottled pectin, stirring constantly. Bring to a full rolling boil and boil for 30 seconds. Remove from the heat, skim, pour quickly into hot, sterile jelly glasses. Add melted paraffin at once to the tops. This makes about 11 medium-sized glasses of jelly.

October Jelly

1 peck grapes
1 quart vinegar
3 medium sour apples

4 tablespoons whole cloves
1/4 cup stick cinnamon
brown sugar

Wash the grapes and remove the stems. Crush. Pour them into an agate kettle. Put all the ingredients but the sugar in with the grapes. Simmer until the fruits are soft. Strain through a flannel jelly bag. Measure the juice and measure an equal amount of sugar. Cook juice for 20 minutes and then add sugar and boil until a little dropped on a cold plate will jell.

HORSERADISH JELLY

1/2 cup grated horseradish
1/2 cup vinegar
3-1/4 cups sugar

1/2 cup liquid pectin (a bottle holds 3/4 cup)

Mix and stir together the vinegar, sugar and horseradish until the sugar has dissolved. Bring the mixture to a boil, then add the pectin immediately. Stirring constantly, bring the kettle again to a full rolling boil and boil for 30 seconds. Remove from the heat, skim, pour and seal. This spicy jelly makes a wonderful garnish for pot roast or cold roast beef.

MINT JELLY — With Vinegar

The traditional accompaniment to lamb.

1 packed cup mint stems and leaves
1 cup water
3-1/2 cups sugar

1/2 cup cider vinegar
1/2 bottle liquid pectin
green food coloring

Wash the mint, put into a pan, and pound with the bottom of a cup or glass. Add the water, sugar, and vinegar and bring to full rolling boil, stirring. Add the pectin and coloring. Continue to stir until a full rolling boil is again attained. Boil quickly for 30 seconds, then skim, remove from heat and strain. Pour into glasses and seal.

MOUNTAIN ASH JELLY

Piquant and rosy-red, this is another excellent meat jelly.

Pick the berries in mid-September, when they are beginning to soften enough to drop off the branches. Wash the berries several times in water to remove any dirt and drain. To each pound of berries, add 1 cup water and cook for 15 minutes, until they reach a pulp. Strain through a jelly bag. Finish as below.

2-2/3 cups mountain ash juice
1-1/3 cups apple juice

4-1/2 cups sugar
1/2 bottle liquid pectin

Mountain ash berries are very tart, almost like persimmons; the addition of apple juice sweetens the jelly and allays the slightly bitter taste of the berries. Stir the sugar into the mixed mountain ash and apple juices and boil this mixture hard for 15 minutes to concentrate the juice. Then add the liquid pectin, bring back to a full rolling boil, and boil for 1 minute, stirring constantly. Remove from the heat, skim, pour, and seal.

PARSLEY JELLY

2 large bunches parsley
3 cups boiling water
2 tablespoons lemon juice

1 box powdered pectin
4-1/2 cups sugar
few drops green food coloring

Wash and chop the parsley. Measure 4 cups chopped parsley into a bowl. Add the boiling water, cover, and let stand 15 minutes. Strain through cheesecloth or a jelly bag.

Measure 3 cups parsley juice into a kettle. Add the lemon juice and pectin. Place over high heat and stir until the mixture comes to a hard boil. Add the sugar and stir. Blend in the green food coloring. Bring to a rolling boil and boil hard 1 minute, stirring constantly. Remove from the heat, skim, pour, and seal. Makes 7 glasses.

PEACH JELLY

3-1/2 cups peach juice   1 package powdered pectin
1/4 cup lemon juice   4-1/2 cups sugar

Mix the peach and lemon juices with the powdered pectin and bring to a full rolling boil over high heat. Stir in the sugar and bring back to the full boil, still stirring. Boil hard for 2 minutes, remove from the heat, skim, pour and seal.

SWEET GREEN PEPPER JELLY

Tastes rather like guava jelly.

3/4 cup seeded and chopped green pepper   1 bottle liquid pectin
1/4 cup seeded and chopped red pepper   1/2-1 teaspoon green food
6 cups sugar   coloring
1-1/2 cups cider vinegar

To best retain juice when chopping peppers, use blender at "chop" speed. Or chop finely in bowl. Bring all ingredients except food color and pectin to a boil and boil for 10 minutes. Add the pectin and bring back to boil. Boil hard for 2 minutes, then remove from heat, skim, and cool. When tepid, stir in the coloring, pour and seal. Makes 4 glasses.

wild plum

WILD PLUM JELLY

3 cups wild plum juice
1 cup green apple juice
7 cups sugar
1/2 bottle liquid pectin

First wash the plums, add water to cover well, and cook thoroughly, 20-25 minutes, or until the plums have split and juiced well. Pour the juice and the plums into the jelly bag and strain. Prepare the apple juice as described in Basic Apple Jelly (see page 12).

Mix the combined juice with the sugar, stirring, and bring to a boil over high heat. Boil hard for 2-3 minutes. Remove from the heat, add liquid pectin, and bring to full boil again, boiling for 1 minute. Remove from the heat, skim, pour into glasses and seal. About 3 pints.

Note: The same proportions may also be used for chokecherry jelly.

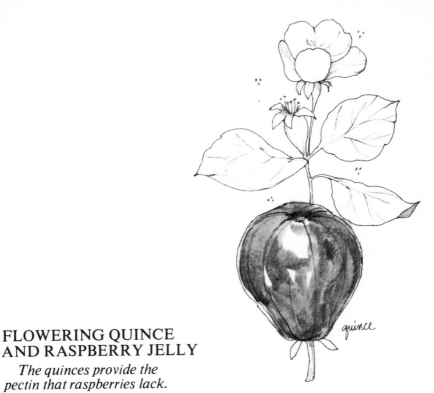

quince

FLOWERING QUINCE AND RASPBERRY JELLY

The quinces provide the pectin that raspberries lack.

Collect flowering quince fruit when it is ready to fall from the branch. Quarter the quinces and remove the cores and seeds. Add water to cover and cook until almost tender. Strain through the jelly bag. To each cup of juice, add 1 cup red raspberry juice, obtained by heating and straining a pint of frozen berries. To each cup of mixed juice, add 1 cup of sugar. Continue as with Basic Apple Jelly (see page 12).

SPICED RHUBARB JELL

2-1/2 lbs. rhubarb, cut up but
  not peeled
1/2 cup cider vinegar
1/2 cup water

1-inch cinnamon stick
3-4 cloves
8 cups sugar
1 bottle liquid pectin

Mix together the rhubarb, vinegar, water and spices (tie the cinnamon and cloves into a cheesecloth bag) and heat to boiling. Cover and simmer for 15 minutes. Strain through the jelly bag.

Measure 4 cups of rhubarb juice and add the sugar to this. Bring to a hard boil, stirring. Add the liquid pectin and boil hard for 1 minute. Remove from the heat and allow to stand 1 minute. Then skim, pour and seal. Serve with meats.

ROSEMARY JELLY

2 tablespoons rosemary
1-1/4 cups boiling water
1/4 cup vinegar

3 cups sugar
food coloring, pink or green
1/2 bottle liquid pectin

Pour the boiling water over the rosemary. Cover and let stand 15 minutes, then strain to remove the herbs.

Measure the infusion into a 3-quart saucepan, adding water if necessary, to make 1 cup. Add the vinegar and sugar and mix.

Place over hottest fire and, while the mixture is coming to a boil, add coloring to the desired shade. As soon as the mixture boils, add the pectin, stirring constantly. Then bring to a full rolling boil and boil hard for 30 seconds.

Remove from the fire, skim, pour quickly. Paraffin the hot jelly at once.

STRAWBERRY JELLY

1 1-lb. box frozen sliced
   strawberries, thawed
1 box powdered pectin

2 cups water
1/4 cup lemon juice
3-1/2 cups sugar

Strain the strawberries through cheesecloth or a jelly bag. Measure out 3/4 cup of syrup. Mix the pectin and water in a kettle and bring to a full rolling boil. Boil hard, stirring constantly, for 1 minute. Reduce the heat to low. Stir in the syrup, lemon juice and sugar. Heat, stirring, until the sugar is thoroughly dissolved. (Do not boil.) Remove from the heat, skim, pour and seal.

(To make a jelly using fresh strawberries, see Strawberry Apple Jelly, page 15.)

2
Jams & Preserves

Sweet and sticky, naturally, both of them, and properly homemade, really delectable. Most people today lump them together, considering, for example, that strawberry *jam* and strawberry *preserves* are one and the same thing. Well, practically. But there is a difference. *Jams* are made from mashed fruit and sugar cooked together to anything from a thick to a runny texture. *Preserves* are made from either whole or cut-up fruit cooked with sugar, and sometimes added pectin, to a texture varying from thick to runny, according to preference.

On Making Jams and Preserves

Jams and preserves are easier and more economical to make than jellies, because they are made of entire fruits, rather than strained juice and can be good thick or runny. Jam is perhaps the easier of the two to prepare. As with jellies, although you can find peach, apricot, strawberry, cherry, plum, raspberry, and occasionally blueberry, blackberry or pineapple jam and, more rarely preserves, commercially, the sugar content is higher, the fruit flavor less than in homemade products, and many classic, old-time jams and preserves are just plain unavailable except through the efforts of the homemaker.

To prepare fruit. Wash and remove the stems and core, if any. Peel if necessary; cherries and berries do not require peeling; things like pears, peaches, quinces, tomatoes, chestnuts and tangerines do. Remove the core from pineapples and shred the fruit, or cut it up fine. Squeeze out tomato seeds. Peel old rhubarb stalks. Pit cherries. For jams — cut up or mash; for preserves — use whole or cut into largish pieces.

Cooking. Make jam or preserves in small batches because in this way, the fruit will cook quickly and the color and flavor will be better preserved. For every cup of fruit, add 3/4 cup of sugar. Four cups of fruit makes a batch of a size easily handled — so you would need 3 cups of sugar per batch, unless otherwise specified by the recipe. Add also 1-2 tablespoons of lemon juice if you are using ripe or sweet fruit. Stir in the sugar until it is dissolved, and bring the mixture to a boil. Keep boiling, stirring often to prevent scorching (which is more apt to happen with jam and preserves than with jelly), for 15-40 minutes (without added pectin), depending on the time it takes for the specific fruit to cook down. Use the candy thermometer to ascertain when the mixture reaches 8 degrees above the boiling point (see directions for Jellies); you can also use the refrigerator test described under Jellies, or see if a spoonful of jam taken out of the pot will hold its shape. If it does, your jam is done.

Take the kettle off the stove and skim. Then stir carefully for 3-4 minutes to keep the fruit from floating on the top.

Pouring and sealing. Ladle out and seal in sterile glasses, label and store as described for Jellies, page 10.

APRICOT JAM

Peel, stone (use a knife or spoon handle at the point of the apricot to push the stone through the stem end) and crush slightly underripe apricots. Reserve the stones. Measure the pulp into the kettle (make sure it has a *flat* bottom) and cook over low heat until tender, adding a little water if necessary and stirring to keep the fruit from scorching. Heat the sugar in the oven (3/4 cup sugar for each cup of pulp). When the fruit is tender, add the sugar and, if the taste is too bland, 1-1/2 teaspoons of lemon juice per cup of pulp. Stir well to dissolve the sugar, bring to a boil, stirring. Continue to boil, stirring as necessary, until the syrup is thick and clear — at the jellying point (see page 8) or almost, depending on the consistency you prefer. This will take 20-40 minutes. Remove from the heat, stir once, skim, then pour into glasses. For a distinctive flavor, crack the stones and add one kernel to each glass before sealing.

apricot

OR TRY THESE 1792 RECIPES —

To make an apricot, or peach, jam.

1. Chuse the ripest apricots, which clean of all hard knobs, spots, and rotten parts. Cut them in small bits in a preserving pan, which you have previously weighed. If you have put four pounds of apricots in it, reduce them by boiling over a gentle fire to two pounds only, which you must find out by weighing pan and fruit together, now and then till you find your right weight. When this is the case, put among your apricots thus reduced to one half, two pounds of lump sugar pulverised, and mix all well for the space of five minutes over the fire, then take all off, let it cool, and pot.

2. This same composition, you may, if you will, put into paste on slates, or in tin moulds. There is not more exquisite eating. You may also, with two or three roasted, or baked, apples, mix a couple of spoonfuls of this marmalade, and make excessive nice tarts with it, or again with pears baked under ashes, nothing can be more delicate.

An apricot jam, after the French way.

1. Chuse such ripe apricots as are fit to eat. Peel their skin off very neatly, and give them a bubble or two in boiling water, so as not to have them dissolve however in the water, and put them a-draining. When done, mash them through a sieve, and let them rest a certain time to evaporate their superfluous moistness.

2. While this is doing, make a syrup with as many pounds of sugar as you have fruit, and take it off from the fire; when the syrup is cooled, put your fruit in, which stir well with a spatula, then put all again on the fire for ten minutes in order to make the fruit take well the sugar. When the jam is done, fine and transparent, you pot it.

BANANA JAM

3 cups mashed bananas
6-1/2 cups sugar
juice and rind of 1 lemon

1/4 teaspoon butter
1 bottle liquid pectin

Combine the first 4 ingredients in a saucepan. Bring to a rolling boil. Add the liquid pectin and boil for 1 minute. Remove from heat, skim, pour, and seal.

BARBERRY JAM

4 quarts barberries
4 lbs. brown sugar
1-1/2 cups water

Cook from 15 to 30 minutes. This jam used to be served with cold meat in grandfather's time.

blackberry

BLACKBERRY JAM

6 cups blackberries
1/2 cup water
6 cups sugar
1 cup orange juice
4 tablespoons lemon juice
1 tablespoon grated orange peel

Cook berries with water until heated through. Rub through sieve and add sugar, fruit juices and grated peel. Cook over low heat until thick. Seal in hot sterilized jars. Makes six 6-ounce glasses.

BLUEBERRY JAM

4-1/2 cups mashed blueberries
   (about 1-1/2 quarts whole
   berries)
7 cups sugar

1 tablespoon lemon juice or vinegar
1 bottle liquid pectin
dab of butter (to reduce foaming)

Mix berries and sugar thoroughly, add lemon juice or vinegar and butter, bring to a boil on high heat and boil 1 minute, stirring occasionally as mixture heats and constantly while it boils. Remove from heat, add pectin, stir briefly and skim off any foam, and pour quickly into hot, sterilized jars. Seal.

SPICED BLUEBERRY JAM

2 lbs. blueberries (4-1/2 cups)	7 cups sugar
1/2 teaspoon cinnamon	juice or grated rind of 1 lemon
1/2 teaspoon cloves	1 bottle liquid pectin

Boil the berries with the sugar, spices and lemon rind for 2 minutes, stirring as needed to prevent scorching. Remove from fire and add the pectin. Skim, pour into sterilized jars, and seal.

TAIYA'S BLUEBERRY-RASPBERRY JAM

4 cups blueberries	4 cups raspberries
7 cups sugar	1 bottle pectin

Crush the berries with a wooden spoon, add the sugar and mix well. Heat to full rolling boil and boil for 1 minute, stirring constantly. Remove from heat, add pectin, skim the top and pour into sterilized jars. Seal with paraffin. Makes eleven 6-ounce glasses of jam.

CHERRY JAM or PRESERVES

Stone sweet cherries. For each batch, place 4 cups cherries (pack tightly) in the kettle. For JAM, crush the fruit; for PRESERVES, mash the cherries lightly in the kettle, just enough to start the juice flowing. Boil the cherries in their juice until tender — about 10 minutes. Add 3 cups oven-heated sugar, stir well to dissolve, and boil 5-7 more minutes. Remove from the heat and let the kettle stand covered, for 2-3 minutes. Then stir, skim if necessary, pour and seal. Makes 4 half-pint jars.

SUN-COOKED CHERRY PRESERVES

Use equal weights of cherries and sugar, i.e. 2 lbs. cherries and 2 lbs. sugar. Mix in a kettle and bring slowly to a boil. Turn over carefully 6 times with a wooden spoon. Then spread the syrupy fruit in shallow platters — a single layer to each platter. Place the platters in a protected place outdoors in the direct rays of the sun. Bring indoors at night. Repeat for 3 days. Then bottle and seal.

CHESTNUT JAM

2 lbs. boiled and shelled chestnuts   1/4 cup water
2 lbs. sugar   1/2 teaspoon vanilla

Chop the chestnuts fairly fine, and place in a saucepan. Add the sugar and water and cook until thick, stirring often. Add vanilla. Spoon into sterilized jelly glasses and seal.

elderberry

ELDERBERRY JAM

4 cups elderberries
7 cups sugar
3/4 cup lemon juice (or vinegar)
1 bottle liquid pectin

Stem the elderberries and place in a kettle with just enough water to keep from scorching (about 1/2 cup). Crush the berries slightly. Add the sugar and lemon juice (or vinegar) and bring quickly to a full rolling boil. Boil for 1 minute, stirring constantly. Then remove from the heat and stir in the pectin. Skim, pour and seal.

SUPER-SMOOTH GRAPE JAM

Wash and pick over grapes that are on the verge of ripeness, including all green ones. Stem the grapes and cook gently with just enough water to prevent burning (about 1/2 cup), mashing them with a wooden spoon, until they are thoroughly softened. Strain this mush through a food mill to remove the seeds and measure.
4 cups grape pulp
3 cups sugar
juice and grated rind of one lemon (optional, but delicious)

Cook gently, stirring to prevent burning, until the mixture is thick enough to spread (about 20 minutes). Pour into hot sterilized glasses and seal with paraffin.

GRAPE-APPLE JAM

Scald 5 lbs. grapes and strain out the juice. Add 6 cups chopped apples. Boil until soft. To each pint of the jam, add a little more than a cup of sugar. Simmer 10 minutes. Pour in jelly jars and seal.

WILD GRAPE SPREAD

Place wild grapes in a crock in alternate layers with granulated sugar — an inch of grapes, an inch of sugar, etc., ending with an inch of sugar on top. Cover with a weighted plate or crock top and leave for some time.

HEAVENLY JAM

3 lbs. ripe peaches   pulp and juice of 2 oranges
3 lbs. sugar   1 3-oz. bottle maraschino cherries
juice and rind of 1 orange

Peel and mash the peaches, discarding the pits. Add the sugar and allow to stand overnight. Then add the orange rind, juice and pulp and the cherries, cut into small pieces. Add the cherry juice also. Cook until thickened. Remove from heat, skim, pour and seal.

PEACH JAM

Use the recipe for Apricot Jam on page 26.

AMBER PEACH PRESERVES

6 lbs. yellow peaches   3/4 cup white vinegar
3 lbs. sugar   1/4 cup water

Wash and dry the peaches and put into the kettle with the sugar, vinegar and water. Cook over a slow fire, chopping the peaches while they cook as you stir with a wooden spoon. Lift out and discard the pits as the peaches are broken apart. (Do not remove the skins — they are absorbed during cooking.) Cook to a "preserves" consistency, leaving the mixture chunky. Pour into sterilized jars or glasses and seal with paraffin.

PEPPER JAM

36 sweet red (or green) peppers   2 cups vinegar
2 tablespoons salt   3 lbs. sugar

Seed and finely chop the peppers. Sprinkle salt over them and let stand for a few hours or overnight. Drain and mix with the vinegar and sugar. Cook over medium heat, stirring until the mixture comes to a boil. Turn down the heat a little and continue to cook, stirring as needed for an hour or so, until thick. Pour and seal.

PINEAPPLE PRESERVES

Slice, peel and core fresh pineapples. Put through the food chopper (coarse disk). Measure pineapple pulp and juice. Put 4 cups at a time in the kettle with 4 cups sugar. Mix well and boil over a medium fire until thick and clear. Remove from fire, skim, pour and seal.

APRICOT-PINEAPPLE-CHERRY JAM

1 lb. dried apricots   1 6-oz. bottle maraschino cherries
1 No. 2 can crushed pineapple   juice 1/2 lemon
sugar

Soak the apricots in cold water to cover for several hours. Then cook until they are soft enough to mash. Drain and mix with the pineapple, cherries (cut up) and cherry and lemon juices. Measure, and add 3/4 cup sugar for every cup of fruit. Cook until thick, stirring frequently. Remove, skim, pour and seal.

VARIATIONS ON Apricot-Pineapple-Cherry Jam

1. Make with pineapple and cherries only.
2. Substitute 2 quarts yellow raspberries for the apricots.
3. Substitute 4-5 bananas, mashed, for the apricots.

CINNAMON PLUM JAM

Cut in half and pit small freestone plums. Measure the fruit. For each cup of fruit use 3/4 cup of sugar, and 2 cinnamon sticks. Mix together in a kettle and cook, stirring constantly, for 1-1/2 to 2 hours, at a simmer. When the mixture has thickened, remove from the stove, skim if necessary, pour and seal. To intensify the flavor, put a stick of cinnamon in each jar before sealing.

GRANDMA'S PUMPKIN PRESERVE

1 medium-sized pumpkin
sugar
1/2 cup lemon juice

1 teaspoon lemon peel
1/2 teaspoon crushed ginger root

Cut the pumpkin in half and scrape out the seeds. Peel off the rind. Cut the pumpkin into small cubes. Measure. Put the diced pumpkin into a kettle with sugar, using 3/4 cup of sugar for every cup of pumpkin. Pour the lemon juice over the pumpkin and sugar, mix all together and let stand overnight. In the morning, add the lemon peel and ginger and simmer until transparent — about one hour. Pour into jars and seal.

RASPBERRY JAM

1 quart raspberries
7 cups sugar
1 bottle liquid pectin

Crush a layer of berries in the kettle, then cover with the remaining berries and sugar. Bring the mixture to a boil over high heat, stirring, and let it boil 1 minute before adding the pectin. Boil for 1 minute after adding the pectin, then remove from the stove, stir, skim, pour and seal.

RHUBARB JAM

5 cups rhubarb, washed and cut up
3 cups sugar
1 3-oz. package strawberry gelatin

Cover the rhubarb with the sugar and let stand overnight. The next morning, bring the mixture to a boil and boil 15 minutes. Remove from the heat and stir in the strawberry gelatin. Pour and seal with paraffin.

JUNE FRUIT JAM

3 cups fresh pineapple, shredded   dash of salt
2 cups rhubarb, cut up   4-1/2 cups sugar
4 cups strawberries, hulled

Cook the pineapple in the kettle over medium heat for 10 minutes, without adding water or other liquid. Add the rhubarb, strawberries and salt and cook for 20 minutes. Add the sugar and bring the mixture to a boil, stirring to prevent scorching and to dissolve the sugar. Boil rapidly, continuing to stir, for 25-30 minutes or until the jam thickens. Skim, pour and seal.

ROSE HIP JAM

Pick rose hips in September when they are red ripe. They are a rich natural source of vitamin C.

Wash 4 cups of rose hips and snip off the ends. Place in an enamel saucepan with a quart of water and bring to a boil. Cook, covered, until tender (about 20 minutes), and purée. Then cook 4 apples, peeled and cored, until soft. Add the rose hip purée and 5 cups sugar. Dissolve the sugar over low heat, then bring the mixture to a boil. Cook until the mixture begins to jell. Pour immediately into glasses and seal.

rose hip

ROSE PETAL JAM

Select rose petals carefully, using the most fragrant. Wash gently. Drain. For each cup of petals, measure 1 cup of sugar, add 1 teaspoon lemon juice, and enough water to dissolve the sugar. Combine the sugar mixture with the petals, and allow to stand for 3 hours, or until melted. Then cook over medium heat until the mixture thickens — about 30 minutes. Stir frequently. Pour into jelly glasses and seal.

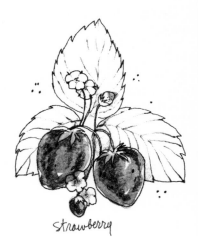
Strawberry

WILD STRAWBERRY JAM

2 lbs. hulled wild strawberries
1-1/2 lbs. sugar

In a preserving kettle place one-fourth of the fruit in a layer. Sprinkle with one-fourth of the sugar. Crush berries and sugar with a potato-masher. This makes plenty of juice so that the jam won't burn. Alternate the next layers of fruit and sugar *without crushing*, until all the fruit and sugar are used. Cook slowly 1-1/2 to 2 hours and stir often. This procedure breaks up the fruit and keeps the mixture from burning. With a gas or electric stove, use an asbestos mat under the kettle.

Test to see if jam is done by taking out a teaspoon of juice and fruit, pour on a cold plate, chill quickly. If thick, it is done. Otherwise cook it longer. Pour in sterilized jars. Cover with paraffin wax when jam is partly cooled. Place tin or glass covers on jars.

REAL OLD-FASHIONED STRAWBERRY PRESERVES

2 lbs. white sugar
2 lbs. strawberries
1/4 teaspoon cream of tartar

Combine the sugar, strawberries and cream of tartar. Let simmer slowly until the sugar melts, then cook briskly for 15-20 minutes. Let stand 24 hours, then pack in sterile jars while cold and seal.

STRAWBERRY SUNSHINE PRESERVES

Using 1-3/4 pounds of sugar to every pound of strawberries, combine sugar and berries in a kettle and bring the mixture slowly to a boil. Boil hard for 20 minutes. Then spread in shallow platters — a single layer of syrupy strawberries to each platter. Place the platters outdoors in the direct rays of the sun. Protect them from insects and other predators with glass and cheesecloth. If the sun shines brightly that day, one day should suffice. Otherwise, repeat the procedure for 2-3 days. Bring inside in evenings. In the morning, bottle cold and seal.

STRAWBERRY-FIG JAM

3 cups mashed figs
3 cups sugar

2 3-oz. packages strawberry gelatin
3/4 cup water

Boil for 3 minutes. Pour into hot jars and seal.

STRAWBERRY-ORANGE JAM

2-1/2 cups frozen strawberries
(2 10-oz. packages)
1 medium orange

1/4 cup water
1/2 box powdered pectin
3-1/2 cups sugar

Thaw the strawberries. Cut the orange in half, remove the seeds and core but do not peel. Grind the orange, using a fine blade. Combine the strawberries, orange and water in a large kettle. Add the pectin and stir well. Place on high heat. Bring quickly to a full rolling boil, stirring constantly. Add the sugar and continue stirring. Heat to a full rolling boil again and, still stirring, boil hard for 1 minute. Remove from the heat; skim and stir alternately for 5 minutes. Pour into jelly jars (4 or 5) up to 1/8 inch from the top. Seal.

QUICK TANGERINE JAM

4 cups tangerine pulp and juice
2 teaspoons grated tangerine rind

2 lemons, pulp and juice
3 cups sugar

Peel the tangerines, separate into sections and remove the seeds and thin skin. Cut the sections into halves, holding them over a bowl as you cut to catch all juice. Measure 4 cups pulp and juice out and combine with the other ingredients. Boil rapidly for 15 minutes, or until syrupy and clear. Cool, then pour into jars and seal. Makes 2 pints.

tomato

GREEN TOMATO PRESERVE

1 lb. green tomatoes
3/4 lb. sugar
1/2 lemon

Slice the tomatoes. Cook the lemon, sliced very thin, in a small amount of water until tender. Then add the tomatoes, drained thoroughly, and the sugar. Cook slowly until the preserve is the consistency of marmalade. Pour into glasses and seal.

RIPE TOMATO PRESERVE

1 lb. red ripe tomatoes, peeled
1 lb. sugar
1 lemon

Follow the directions for Green Tomato Preserve (above).

YELLOW TOMATO PRESERVES

| 4 cups yellow tomatoes, skinned | 4 cups sugar |
| 1 lemon | 3/4 cup water |

Put the sugar and water in a kettle, stir to dissolve and boil to the soft-ball stage (234°F). Add the tomatoes and boil slowly for 3 hours. The last half hour, add the lemon, thinly sliced. Skim, pour and seal hot.

WINTER JAM

1 1-lb. can water-packed pitted
  cherries
1 10-oz. package frozen sliced
  strawberries, thawed

1/8 teaspoon salt
3 tablespoons fresh lemon juice
4-1/2 cups sugar
1/2 bottle liquid pectin

Drain the cherries, reserving the juice. Chop fine, then measure and add enough cherry juice to make 2 cups. Combine with the strawberries in a kettle. Add the lemon juice and sugar and mix well. Bring to a full rolling boil. Boil hard for 1 minute, stirring constantly. Remove from the heat and immediately stir in the pectin. Skim and stir to prevent floating fruit. Pour and seal.

3
Conserves &
Marmalades

These are both fancy jams. Conserves are usually a rich mixture of different fruits, often combined with nuts or raisins. Marvelous with bland foods such as rice or hot cereal. Marmalades are softly jellied jams containing pieces of fruit and peel. Again, for the most part, except for orange marmalade, you would be hard put to obtain these preserves in the market. Not only are they fun and tasty to have on hand at home, but they make, in common with all homemade preserves, fantastic Christmas presents. Priceless — because they cannot be bought.

Conserves are made basically like preserves; marmalades are made more like jellies, but with sliced, ground or diced fruit rather than clear juices.

Conserves

APPLE AND PEACH CONSERVE

2 cups tart apples, cored and
   diced
2 cups peaches, peeled, stoned
   and diced

1/2 cup corn syrup
1/2 cup sugar
1/2 orange, grated rind and juice
1/4 cup chopped walnuts

Add just enough water to the fruit to cover it; cook until tender.
Add the syrup, sugar, orange juice and rind, and cook the mixture
until it is clear and thick. Add the walnuts, and turn the conserve into
clean glasses. Cover with paraffin when cold.

CRAB APPLE CONSERVE

3 quarts crab apples
3 oranges
3 quarts sugar
1 teaspoon cinnamon

1 pint cider vinegar
1 teaspoon cloves
1 lb. seedless raisins

Remove cores of crab apples. Cut crab apples in small pieces. Grind
the peel of the oranges. Mix all of the ingredients together. Let stand
about 24 hours. Add juice of the oranges. Cook mixture until it
becomes thick like marmalade. Bottle and seal.

CRAB APPLE PEACH CONSERVE

2 cups chopped, unpared crab
   apples (cored and pitted)
2 cups chopped peeled peaches

1/2 cup lemon juice
3 cups sugar

Combine the ingredients and cook slowly until the apples are
transparent, about 30 minutes. Remove from heat. Stir and skim
alternately for 5 minutes. Pour into hot sterilized glasses. Seal.

BLUEBERRY CONSERVE

2 oranges
juice of 1 lemon
1/2 cup water

1 quart blueberries
sugar

Peel the oranges. Cut the rind into thin strips. Remove the white,
inner skin and cut the fruit into thin slices. Add the lemon juice,
water and blueberries. Bring to a boil, then measure. Add to the
measured fruit mixture in the kettle 2/3 as much sugar as fruit.
Simmer until the mixture is thick. Pour and seal.

CHERRY-PINEAPPLE CONSERVE

4 cups tart red cherries
1 cup canned crushed pineapple, drained

3 cups sugar
1/2 cup blanched chopped almonds

Wash and stone the cherries. Grind them in a food mill and measure. Put into a kettle with the pineapple and sugar. Cook rapidly until the mixture is thick and clear. Stir in the almonds. Pour into sterilized jars and seal.

CHERRY-RASPBERRY CONSERVE

3 cups tart red cherries
3 cups raspberries
4-1/2 cups sugar

1/2 cup chopped blanched almonds (or other nuts)

Cook the cherries in a very little water, about 1/3 cup, until tender. Add the raspberries and sugar and cook until the mixture is thick and clear. Stir in the nuts and cook 5 more minutes. Pour and seal.

cherry

CRANBERRY CONSERVE

1 orange
1 cup water
1/2 cup sugar
1 lb. cranberries

2 cups water
2 cups sugar
1 cup seeded raisins
1/2 cup walnuts

Cut up the orange and rind in small pieces and remove the seeds. Add 1 cup of water and 1/2 cup sugar and simmer until the rind is tender. Cook the cranberries in 2 cups of water. Add 2 cups sugar, then the raisins. Continue to cook until the mixture thickens, then add the orange rind and the nuts. Pour into jars and seal.

GOLDEN CONSERVE

3 lbs. Burbank plums, pitted and
    quartered
2 Valencia oranges, rind and all,
    seeded, sliced very thin and slivered

5 lbs. sugar
12 oz. golden seedless raisins
8 oz. slivered almonds

Boil the plums, oranges, raisins and sugar together until the mixture is thick and clear. Remove from the fire and add the almonds. Ladle into sterilized jars and seal with paraffin.

GOOSEBERRY-RHUBARB CONSERVE

1-1/2 lbs. gooseberries
1 lb. rhubarb

4 cups sugar
1/2 cup chopped walnuts

Wash the fruit, removing the stems and tails from the gooseberries and cutting the rhubarb into short lengths. Put the fruit into a kettle with the sugar and boil until thick, stirring as needed. Add the nuts. Remove from the heat, pour and seal.

GRAPE CONSERVE

5 lbs. grapes
5 lbs. sugar

1 lb. seeded raisins
2 oranges

Wash and skin the grapes, reserving the skins. Cook the pulp until it softens, then sieve to remove the seeds. Add to the pulp the grape skins, oranges (peeled, seeded, and sliced into small pieces), grated orange rind, sugar, raisins, and just enough water to keep from burning. Cook, stirring, until thick. Pour and seal.

NEW ENGLAND FRUIT CONSERVE

1 quart cantaloupe, diced
3 cups peaches, diced
juice of 2 lemons
juice of 1 orange
1 cup English walnuts, chopped
4-1/2 cups sugar

Cook the above (except the nuts) together until thick and clear. Add the nuts and turn into sterilized glasses. Seal.

PEACH CONSERVE

4 cups diced peaches (12 medium peaches)
4 cups sugar
juice and peel of 1 orange
1 cup chopped walnuts
1 small bottle maraschino cherries, minced and drained

Cook the orange peel in a little water for 10 minutes. Drain. Scrape off the white part and chop the peel finely. Add to the sugar, peaches and orange juice and cook until quite thick. When almost done, add the walnuts and chopped cherries.

PEACH-PINEAPPLE CONSERVE

5 cups peaches, diced
5 cups sugar
2 cups crushed pineapple
1/2 — 1 cup chopped nuts (hickories, pecans, or walnuts)
1 medium jar maraschino cherries and juice (For a pink conserve, mince the cherries. For a yellow conserve, chop in halves.)

Mix the peaches with the sugar and pineapple and allow to stand for 15 minutes. Then boil gently until thick and clear. Add the cherries, cherry juice and nuts. Cook 1 minute longer. Pour and seal.

PEAR CONSERVE

6 cups sliced pears, cored but not peeled
7 cups sugar
1 lemon, thinly sliced
1/2 bottle liquid pectin
1/2 cup chopped nuts

Mix the pears, sugar and lemon and boil until the pears are clear. Add the pectin and boil for 1 minute. Then add the nuts. Pour and seal.

PLUM GUMBO

5 lbs. plums
2 lbs. seeded raisins
3 oranges

5 lbs. sugar
2 cups chopped nuts

Wipe the plums, remove the stones and cut into pieces. Chop the raisins fine. Wipe the oranges, remove seeds, and cut into thin slices crosswise. Put the fruit into the kettle, add the sugar and bring to a boil. Simmer until the mixture is the consistency of marmalade. Add the nuts, pour and seal.

PUMPKIN CONSERVE

3 lbs. pumpkin, peeled and chopped
3 lbs. sugar
1/2 cup vinegar
rind of 1 orange

pulp of 2 oranges
juice of 2 lemons
1/2 cup chopped walnuts
1 cup raisins

Cook the pumpkin with the sugar and vinegar and boil for 30 minutes. Chop up the orange rind and pulp and the raisins, add to the pumpkin mixture and cook for 30 minutes more. Pour into sterilized glasses and seal with paraffin. Delicious with roast beef.

GRANDMOTHER'S RASPBERRY CONSERVE

2 cups red raspberries
2 cups red currants (or raisins)
4 cups cut-up rhubarb
2 cups chopped walnuts

2 oranges, sliced very thinly
2 lemons, sliced very thinly
sugar

Wash and drain the fruit. Measure for each batch, 4 cups of fruit into the kettle and add 2 cups sugar. Cook slowly, stirring often, until the mixture is as thick as jelly. Add the nuts. Pour into jars and seal.

RHUBARB CONSERVE

2 lbs. rhubarb
2 oranges
1 lemon

3-1/2 cups sugar
1/2 cup chopped nuts

Grate the rind of the 2 oranges and the lemon. Extract the juices. Wash the rhubarb and cut into 1/2-inch pieces. Combine all the ingredients except the nuts and cook slowly, stirring constantly, until the mixture is thick and clear — about 30 minutes. Add the nuts and cook 5 minutes longer. Ladle into glasses and seal with paraffin.

RHUBARB-FIG CONSERVE

3-1/2 lbs. rhubarb
1/2 lb. figs
3 lbs. sugar

1/3 cup candied orange peel
2 lemons, thinly sliced
1 cup blanched slivered almonds

Cut the rhubarb into 1/2-inch pieces. Wash the figs and cut them into strips. Mix together the rhubarb, figs, sugar, lemons and orange peel. Cover and let stand 1 hour. Heat slowly to boiling. Add the almonds. Remove the cover and boil rapidly, stirring, until thick — about 30 minutes. Turn into sterile jars and seal.

ROSE CONSERVE

2 cups sugar	1 whole clove
2 cups water	1 quart rose petals

Gather the petals when they are in full bloom and dewy fresh. Spread on a white towel to dry.

Boil the sugar and water together until a candy thermometer registers 240°F, or the syrup is well thickened. Add the clove, then the petals, a cupful at a time. Simmer for about 5 minutes, then skim out the petals with a perforated spoon. Place the petals in small, sterilized jars. Remove the clove and bring the syrup to a full rolling boil, then pour it into the jars over the petals. Let cool before sealing.

Uses for Rose Conserve

1. Serve with crisp crackers and cream cheese, for dessert.
2. Add 1 teaspoon Rose Conserve to a steaming cup of tea.
3. Use as a topping for ice cream or plain puddings.
4. Spread between thin slices of buttered bread.
5. Use a bit to color and flavor a glass of icy milk.
6. Fill hollowed-out cupcakes with Rose Conserve, then frost over with sweetened, pink-tinted whipped cream.
7. Use Rose Conserve between cake layers, then frost the cake with plain Seven Minute Icing, and decorate with candy roses.
8. Mix Rose Conserve and fluffy cottage cheese with just a bit of mayonnaise for a fruit salad topping.
9. Use a spoonful in the center of sugar cookies.
10. Spread a thin layer of Rose Conserve over a plain, sheet cake. Cover with slices of vanilla ice cream, then refreeze together and serve in slices.

Marmalades

AMBER MARMALADE

3 oranges
3 lemons
1 grapefruit

water
sugar

Slice off the ends of the fruits and quarter them. Remove the seeds. Cut the quarters into very thin shreds or slices. Measure and add three times the amount of water as fruit. Combine the water with the fruit and let stand in a covered bowl overnight. Next morning boil the mixture for 10 minutes and let stand again in the covered bowl overnight. Measure again and add an equal amount of sugar. Boil steadily until the mixture reaches the jellying point (see page 8). Pour into jars and seal.

APPLE MARMALADE

5 lbs. sugar
2-1/2 cups water
2 oranges, seeded

2 lemons, seeded
5 lbs. tart apples, peeled and cored
juice of 1 lemon

Heat the sugar and water together until the sugar is dissolved. Slice the oranges, lemons and apples very thin and add the lemon juice. Put into the kettle with the syrup and boil very slowly until thick — about 1 hour and 15 minutes. Turn into sterilized jars, cool, and seal.

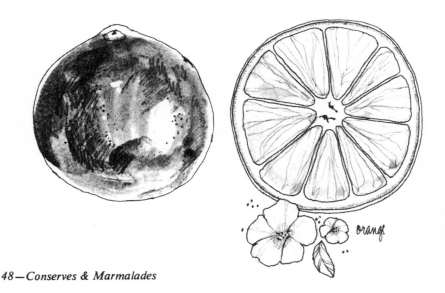

orange

APRICOT MARMALADE

1 lb. dried apricots
1-1/2 cups sugar
1 tablespoon grated lemon rind

1 tablespoon grated orange rind
6 tablespoons lemon juice

Soak the apricots overnight in cold water barely to cover. Next day, cover and cook in the same water until the apricots are puffy and tender. Press through a sieve, liquid and all. To 2 cups pulp, add the sugar, lemon juice and rinds. Cook over medium high heat, stirring constantly, until thick and waxy — about 15 minutes. Pour into hot sterilized glasses and seal with paraffin.

APRICOT-PINEAPPLE MARMALADE

1 lb. dried apricots
2 cups sugar

1 No. 2 can crushed pineapple
6-1/2 cups water

Cut the apricots into pieces with scissors and soak overnight. Next day, cook the apricots in the same water until tender. Drain. Mix the sugar, pineapple and apricots with the 6-1/2 cups water. Cook, stirring frequently, until the mixture thickens. Remove from heat, pour and seal.

CARROT MARMALADE

2-1/2 cups cooked chopped
   carrots
4 cups sugar

juice and chopped rind of 1 lemon
juice and chopped rind of 1 orange

Boil the chopped rind in a little water until tender. Add the carrots, orange and lemon juices and the sugar. Cook until thick, stirring. Pour and seal.

CHRISTMAS MARMALADE

3 oranges
1 large lemon
1 No. 2 can crushed pineapple
2 small bottles maraschino cherries

1/2 cup water
6 cups sugar
(1/2 cup chopped walnuts)

Remove the seeds from the oranges and lemon and put through a food mill. Mix the pulp with the pineapple, water and sugar. Cook for 45 minutes. Add the cherries, drained and cut into small pieces. Bring to a boil and add the optional nuts. Pour and seal.

EASTER MARMALADE

6 grapefruit
6 oranges
6 lemons
sugar

water
1-1/2 lbs. whole candied cherries
1 lb. candied pineapple, cut up
1/2 lb. preserved ginger, cut up

Peel the rind from oranges, lemons and grapefruit. Put the grapefruit rind through a food mill. Slice the orange and lemon rind into *thin* strips, 1/2 inch long. Remove the seeds from the fruit and slice thinly, crosswise. Measure the fruit and rind and add to it an equal amount of water. Let stand overnight. Next morning, cook until the rind is tender, and let stand overnight again. The third day, measure the mixture again, and add an equal amount of sugar. Cook for about 1-1/2 hours, stirring frequently. Add the candied fruit and ginger and continue cooking until the mixture sheets from the spoon (see page 8). Pour into hot jars, filling to 1/4 inch from the top. Seal with paraffin. Makes about 17 pints.

HONEY MARMALADE

4 large oranges, unpeeled
1 lemon unpeeled
1 grapefruit, peeled

3 cups water
1-3/4 cups sugar
1 cup honey

Cut the fruit into sections, remove the seeds, and put the fruit through a food grinder, using the medium blade. There should be 3 cups of pulp. Add the water, sugar, and honey and cook until the mixture reaches the jellying point (see page 8). Pour and seal. This marmalade is best made in small quantities for immediate use.

ORANGE MARMALADE

5 large navel oranges
1 lemon
water

sugar
lemon juice

Cut off the thick ends of the oranges and lemon. Remove the seeds from the lemon. Then cut the fruit in round slices, very thin. Halve and quarter the slices. Measure the fruit. For each pint of fruit, add 3 pints water. Let stand for 24 hours. Boil for 45 minutes, then let stand another 24 hours. Measure again, and add 3 cups of sugar and the juice of one lemon for every 2 cups of the fruit mixture. Boil for 45 minutes. Pour and seal.

The marmalade made from this grand old recipe is sweet, not bitter.

PEACH MARMALADE

1/2 orange, seeded
1 lemon, halved and seeded
6 tablespoons water
1/8 teaspoon baking soda

1-1/2 cups diced peaches
3-3/4 cups sugar
1/2 cup liquid pectin

Put the skin of the orange half and one lemon half (you want a peel about 1/8 inch thick) through a food mill, using the fine blade. Add the water and baking soda and simmer for 10 minutes in a covered pan. Squeeze the juice from the orange half and both halves of the lemon. Add the pulp and juice to the cooked rind and simmer, covered, for 20 minutes longer. Combine in a kettle the peaches and the simmered fruit. Add the sugar and bring to a boil, stirring constantly. Boil for 5 minutes. Stir in the liquid pectin. Skim and stir for 5 minutes. Pour and seal.

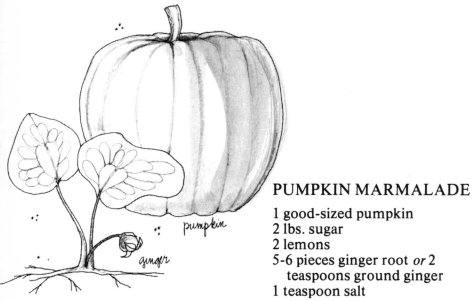

pumpkin

ginger

PUMPKIN MARMALADE

1 good-sized pumpkin
2 lbs. sugar
2 lemons
5-6 pieces ginger root *or* 2
    teaspoons ground ginger
1 teaspoon salt

Peel the pumpkin and scoop out the inside. Discard the rind and seeds. Cut the flesh into cubes. Measure out 3 quarts of pumpkin cubes into a bowl, add the sugar and let stand overnight. Next morning, there will be a lot of juice. Take out the pumpkin fruit and set aside. Add to the juice the lemons (seeded and cut up, rind and all), ginger and salt. Boil this mixture hard, adding the pumpkin fruit slowly as it boils. Cook until the pumpkin is clear. Pour and seal. Wonderful on hot toast.

SPICED PRUNE MARMALADE

1 lb. prunes
1 cup vinegar
1-1/2 cups sugar

1/2 teaspoon cloves
1 tablespoon cinnamon

Soak the prunes for 3 hours and simmer for 60 minutes in the same water. Drain, reserving the liquid. Remove the pits and cut the prunes in small pieces. Return to the stove with the reserved liquid. Add the vinegar, sugar and spices. Simmer until thick, stirring as needed. Pour and seal. Delicious with cold sliced meat.

RASPBERRY-CURRANT MARMALADE

8 cups raspberries
4 cups currants

9 cups sugar

Wash and drain red or black fruit before measuring. Stem and crush the currants. Cook slowly until the juice flows freely. Add the raspberries and bring to a boil. Add the sugar and boil hard to the jellying point (see page 8). Pour and seal.

RHUBARB MARMALADE

4 lbs. rhubarb
1 lb. seeded raisins
2 oranges

1 lemon
3-1/2 to 4 lbs. sugar

Skin the rhubarb and cut into 1/2-inch pieces. Cover with sugar and leave overnight. Remove the peel from the oranges and lemon in quarters. Cook in boiling water until soft. Drain and scrape off the white part from the peel. Cut the peel into strips. Squeeze the oranges and lemon to obtain the juice and pulp, being careful to remove the seeds. In the morning, boil the rhubarb with the raisins and sugar slowly for 30 minutes. Then add the peel, pulp, and juice of the oranges and lemon. Simmer for 1 hour longer, or until thick enough to suit.

RHUBARB-PINEAPPLE MARMALADE

4 cups rhubarb, cut up
1/2 cup water
1 cup crushed canned pineapple,
    drained

7 cups sugar
(1/2 cup chopped walnuts)

Cook the cut rhubarb in the water until tender. Add the pineapple and sugar and cook until the syrup sheets off the spoon — about 20 minutes. Stir in the optional nuts. Pour and seal.

TOMATO MARMALADE

3 cups ripe tomatoes
3 cups sugar

juice, pulp and rind of 1 orange
juice, pulp and rind of 1 lemon

Peel the tomatoes. Combine with the other ingredients in a kettle and cook until the mixture is ready to jell (see page 8). Pour and seal.

GREEN TOMATO MARMALADE

1/2 peck (4 quarts) green
tomatoes, not skinned
12 cups sugar

1/2 lb. citron, cut in pieces
4 lemons, cut fine

Cut the tomatoes in small pieces, cover with boiling water and cook for 5 minutes. Drain off the water. Put the tomatoes in a kettle with the lemons, citron and sugar. Boil all together for 1-1/2 hours, stirring frequently. Pour and seal.

WATERMELON MARMALADE

4 cups chopped watermelon rind
4 apples, peeled, cored and chopped
2 oranges, chopped without peeling,
and seeded

juice of 3 lemons
4 cups sugar
2-1/2 cups water

Mix all the ingredients thoroughly and boil until thick or about 2-1/2 hours. Stir from time to time to prevent sticking. Pour into sterilized jars while hot. Seal. Makes six 6-ounce jars.

watermelon

4 Fruit Butters, Honeys & Leathers

Butters and honeys are spreads — essentially they are both thick fruit sauces made with sugar and sometimes quite highly seasoned — with ginger, cloves, lemon juice, cinnamon, and the like. Butters are opaque, honeys clear. Of these tempting old-fashioned recipes, only apple butter can be obtained outside the home, but as Deanna F. Darling notes on the next page, "store-bought spread just can't match . . . real, honest-to-goodness homemade apple butter."

Spread butters on fresh bread or toast. Try honeys this way too, or on hot biscuits and popovers, but also remember they make a *very special* topping for ice cream, waffles and pancakes.

Fruit leather, a sweetened purée of fruit dried into flat sheets in the sun, is one other way of preserving the fleeting fruits of summer through the long winter. A staple and favorite snack in Grandmother's day, leather seems now to be reappearing on pantry shelves after a long absence.

A Word About Fruit Butters

from Deanna F. Darling

*Unlike jams and jellies, fruit butters require very little sweetening and
there is no trick to cooking them — it just takes time. . . .*

Fruit butters are a traditional and increasingly popular method of
preserving fruits. They require much less sweetening than jams,
jellies or preserves, and can be made in very large quantities.

Fruit butters have a long history. In Germany the word *latwert*
originally meant prune or pear butter, which the people of the
Rhenish Palatinate made to keep these fruits over the winter months.
It took up to 48 hours to prepare these butters and the preparation
became the occasion for a folk festival.

The descendants of these Germans, the Pennsylvania Dutch,
brought *latwert* with them when they came to America. In this
country, the term came to be associated with apple butter because the
Pennsylvania Dutch made such huge quantities of it, stirring apples
and cider in vat-sized kettles over an open fire. As you may well
imagine, this, too, was a festive event, one often used as an excuse
for courting. Like many other once-regional specialties, apple butter
has been made available to most parts of the country by modern
transportation and improved marketing facilities; but store-bought
spread just can't match the taste of real, honest-to-goodness
homemade apple butter.

Although apple butter is the one you are most likely to find in your
cookbook, butters can be made from almost any fruit. Make fruit
butter only when you can spend the entire day in the kitchen, perhaps
while you're baking or doing other canning, because it is important
than you stir the butter frequently to avoid scorching.

Fruit butters will thicken naturally as they cook, so you don't have
to be concerned about testing for pectin or acid. Since they are less
delicate than jellies you don't have to worry about taking them off the
stove at exactly the right moment for fear they won't jell. The test for
thickness of a fruit butter is simple, fast and easy: put a dab of the
butter on a plate, and let it set for a few minutes. If the dab does not
separate — that is, if you don't notice liquid at the edges of the drop
— the butter is ready to be put up in sterilized jars.

Although fruit butters made with sugar or honey have been known
to keep for years without spoiling, since bacteria cannot grow well in
sweet foods, it is best to can your butters. You can do this by

processing both pint and quart jars in a boiling-water bath for 10 minutes.

A cast-iron pot slung on a tripod over an outdoor fire is the best way I know to make butters — and the most pleasurable way of getting the family and friends to participate, but unfortunately this method is not suited to most people's lives today. To make butters on the stove you should have a large kettle or pot with a heavy bottom. If you plan to make large quantities it might be worthwhile to invest in a large stainless steel stockpot. Stockpots come in various sizes and you can choose whichever suits your needs and budget. You will often get a good price on a second-hand stockpot at a restaurant supply store.

Aluminum stockpots are considerably cheaper than those made from stainless steel, but don't be tempted by the lower price unless you plan to use it only for the boiling-water-bath processing. The acids in fruits react with the aluminum and cause both a color and flavor change in the butters. The metals in stainless steel are stable and will not react with the acids in fruit or other foods. A thick-bottomed pot is best because a thin bottom will not conduct heat evenly. If you have a thin-bottomed pot, buy an asbestos pad for the burner and place it under the pot to spread the heat evenly and prevent hot spots from developing.

Some people prefer to bake their fruit butters in the oven. Again, stainless steel is good for this. Glass casserole dishes are also good, as are enamel roasting pans. Make sure the pan you use is large enough to spread a shallow layer of butter. A thick layer will cook up much too slowly.

I add honey to taste when the butter has finished cooking down, rather than while the fruit is cooking. Honey does have a definite flavor of its own which will slightly alter the flavor of the butters, so many people prefer to sweeten with sugar. If sugar is used it must be boiled with the fruit and cannot be added at the end.

If your fruits are ripe or slightly overripe the natural sugars in them are at their peak and you may not need any extra sweetener. If you add the honey before tasting the finished product, it may turn out too sweet.

The ingredients of a few of the recipes are given in parts rather than in actual measurements, like cups or pounds. This is so you may easily adjust the quantities and use just the amount of fruit that you have on hand.

*　*　*　*

BASIC APPLE BUTTER

Use 3 parts cider, 2 parts apples. Peel and core apples, and slice very thin. Put the cider in a large pot and bring to a boil. Add the apples slowly, being careful not to splatter yourself. Allow apples and cider to come to a boil, then simmer, stirring frequently to prevent sticking.

When the apple butter has begun to thicken considerably, the slices will start to fall apart as you stir. Once the butter is thick enough so that it doesn't separate, test it for sweetness. Add honey to taste. You can also add spices. I leave some as is, and to some I add cinnamon, allspice and ground cloves to taste. Bring the new mixture to a boil, then put into hot, sterilized jars, leaving 1/4-inch headspace. Screw the lids on tightly.

Process pints and quarts for 10 minutes in a boiling-water bath. Remove from heat and seal the jars, if necessary. Cool them on a wire rack and store in a cool, dark place.

OVEN-BAKED APPLE BUTTER

Peel and cut apples up in small pieces. Cover the apples with hot water and cook until tender. Put through a sieve and measure the pulp. Add 3/4 cup sugar to each cup of pulp. For each gallon of pulp, add 1/2 teaspoon cloves and 2 teaspoons cinnamon. Bake the spiced pulp in the oven at 325°F, stirring every 15 or 20 minutes, until thick. When baked to desired thickness, put into hot sterilized jars and process as for Basic Apple Butter.

HAYDN S. PEARSON'S APPLE BUTTER

Boil 4 quarts of cider until it becomes 2 quarts. Add 4 quarts of apples, pared, cored and quartered. Cook over low fire 3 or 4 hours. Add:

3 cups sugar	3/4 teaspoon nutmeg
3 teaspoons cinnamon	3/4 teaspoon allspice
1/4 teaspoon cloves	

Stir almost constantly until the sugar is dissolved and all blended well with cider and apples. Bottle and seal immediately.

QUICK APPLE BUTTER

Peel, quarter and core the apples. Cook with just enough water to prevent sticking. Put through a food mill or sieve to make pulp.

5 cups apple pulp	3 cups sugar
1/4 cup vinegar	1 teaspoon cinnamon (or 1 dozen red hots)

Simmer until thick. Put in sterilized jars and process. About 4 small jars.

APRICOT BUTTER

Cut as much fruit as you have in halves, remove the pits, and place in a large kettle with enough water to prevent scorching. Cook until tender. When the apricots are tender, put them through a fruit press or a sieve. Cook the pulp until thick, stirring frequently to prevent scorching. When the butter is thick sweeten with honey, if necessary.

Pour into hot, sterilized jars. Screw the lids on tightly. Process pints and quarts for 10 minutes in boiling-water bath. Remove the jars from the canner and complete seals, if necessary. Cool on wire rack and store in a cool, dry, dark place.

BLUEBERRY BUTTER

8 cups fresh blueberries	1 teaspoon ground allspice
8 large green cooking apples, peeled, cored and sliced	1 teaspoon ground mace
8 cups sugar	1 teaspoon nutmeg

Combine all the ingredients in a large saucepan. Bring to a boil, lower heat and simmer for 1 hour, stirring occasionally. Cook until mixture is thick. Spoon the hot mixture into sterilized glasses. Process and complete the seal if necessary. Store jars in a cool dry place. Makes 8 pints.

SPICED GRAPE BUTTER

1-1/2 lbs. stemmed Concord grapes	2-1/4 cups sugar
1 tablespoon grated orange rind	1/2 teaspoon cinnamon
1 cup water	1/4 teaspoon cloves

Wash the grapes and skin. Reserve the skins. Cook the pulp until it softens, then sieve to remove seeds. Add the orange peel and water and cook 10 minutes. Add the grape skins and heat to boiling. Then put in the sugar and spices and cook until thick, stirring as needed. Process in hot sterilized glasses. Makes six 6-ounce glasses.

PEACH BUTTER

Use 3 parts sliced peaches, 1 part water. Peel the peaches and remove the pits. (For freestone peaches, scald for 1 minute to remove the skins.) Place the peaches in large pot and cook until soft, shaking pot frequently to prevent sticking. (It is better if you divide your peach butter up among several pots for this part of the operation.) When the fruit is tender, put it through a sieve or fruit press. Turn the purée into a shallow roasting pan or pans and cook, uncovered, in the oven for 1 hour at 325°F. Continue cooking, stirring every 15 to 20 minutes, until the butter is thick, fine-textured and a rich reddish-amber color.

When it has reached this stage, take it out of the oven. Ladle into hot, sterilized jars. Screw on the lids tightly. Process pints and quarts 10 minutes in a boiling-water bath. Remove jars from canner and complete seals if necessary. Cool jars on a wire rack and store in a cool, dry, dark place.

PEAR BUTTER

Use 1 part water, 2 parts apple cider, 3 parts pears. Peel, core and slice pears. Put the cider and water in a big pot and bring to a boil. Add the pears slowly, being careful not to splatter. Allow pears and cider to come to a boil, then simmer, stirring frequently to prevent sticking.

When the pear butter has begun to thicken considerably, the slices will fall apart as you stir. Simmer until the pear butter is a thick, deep-dark-brown mass. Test to see if it has thickened enough. If it needs sweetening, use honey and sweeten to taste. If you wish, add cinnamon, ground cloves, and allspice to taste. Bring the mixture to a boil, then put in hot, sterilized jars, leaving headspace. Screw the lids on tightly.

Process pints and quarts for 10 minutes in a boiling-water bath. Remove from heat and seal jars, if necessary. Cool on a wire rack and store in a cool, dark place.

PLUM BUTTER

Wash the plums and remove all blemishes. Put in a kettle and add enough water so that the plums are just covered. Cook until tender. Put through a food mill or fruit press to remove pits and skins. Measure the pulp and add 1/2 cup of honey for each cup of plum pulp, if desired. Return to heat and cook until thick. Pack in hot, sterilized jars leaving a 1/4-inch headspace. Screw the lids on tightly. Process pints and quarts 10 minutes in boiling-water bath. Remove the jars from canner and complete the seals, if necessary. Cool upright on wire rack and store in a cool, dry, dark place.

PRUNE BUTTER

Use 1 lb. prunes, 1/2 cup white or cider vinegar. Rinse prunes, cover with water, bring to a boil, and then reduce heat and simmer until tender. Cool slightly. Remove pits (if you are not using the pitted prunes). Then put the prunes through a fruit press. Add the vinegar. You can add spices to the butter now, if you wish. I use 1/4 teaspoon powdered cloves, 1/4 teaspoon grated nutmeg, 1/2 teaspoon powdered allspice. Cook until thick; sweeten with honey.

Pour into hot sterilized jars leaving a 1/4-inch headspace. Screw lids on tightly and process in boiling-water bath for 10 minutes. Remove jars from water bath, complete seals if necessary, and cool upright on wire racks. Store in a cool, dark place.

QUINCE BUTTER

Apples may be substituted for quince in this recipe.

Core and slice the fruit and put in a large kettle with just enough water to cover. Simmer until soft, stirring often. Put the soft fruit through a food mill and measure. Add one-half as much sugar as you have fruit. Simmer this mixture until thick, stirring frequently to prevent sticking. Add cinnamon, cloves and allspice to taste while the mixture is cooking. Test for thickness. When done fill hot pint jars and seal immediately.

TOMATO BUTTER

Take 5 lbs. tomatoes. Peel and cover with vinegar. Let stand overnight. Drain well. Make a syrup of 1/2 pint vinegar, 1-1/2 lbs. brown sugar, and 1/4 teaspoon red pepper. Place 1/2 tablespoon each of cloves, cinnamon, and allspice in a bag in the syrup. Add 1/2 tablespoon salt. After syrup boils, put in tomatoes and boil until thick.

Honeys

CLOVER HONEY

5 lbs. sugar
3 cups water
1 teaspoon powdered alum *or*
   crystal alum the size of a cherry

40 white clover blossoms
24 red clover blossoms
16 pink rose petals

Combine the sugar and water and boil together until the mixture is clear. Add the alum and boil for 2 minutes longer. Pour this syrup over the clover blossoms and rose petals and let stand 10 minutes. Strain, pour into glasses and seal with paraffin.

GINGER PEAR HONEY

5 lbs. pears
2-1/2 oz. Canton ginger *or*
   1 tablespoon powdered ginger

2-1/2 lbs. sugar
2 lemons

Peel, core and slice the pears. Put the fruit through a sieve or food mill. Add the ginger and sugar and let stand overnight. Next morning, add the lemons, seeded and cut into small pieces, rind and all. Bring to a boil, stirring to prevent scorching. Simmer slowly until thick — about 3 hours. Strain and pour into hot sterilized jars. Seal with paraffin. About eight 6-ounce glasses. Wonderful over pancakes or vanilla ice cream.

PEACH HONEY

4 cups peach pulp
8 cups sugar

Skin and stone ripe peaches and mash or put through a food mill. Cook, stirring over low heat to dissolve the sugar. Bring to a boil, still stirring. Simmer until thick and clear — about 30 minutes. Pour into glasses and seal with paraffin.

QUINCE HONEY

5 quinces   4 cups water
3 lbs. sugar   (1 teaspoon lemon juice)

Peel and core the quinces and put through a coarse meat grinder. Boil the sugar and water together for 10 minutes. Add the ground quinces and let simmer slowly for about 1 hour, or until the honey turns pink. (If your quinces are very ripe, add the teaspoon of lemon juice 10 minutes after you put the quinces in the pot.)

TOMATO HONEY

For each pound of ripe tomatoes allow the grated rind of 1 lemon. Cut the tomatoes into small pieces, add the rind and cook until quite thick. Press through a purée sieve, measure the pulp and for each pint add 1 cup sugar, 1 cup honey and the juice of 1-1/2 lemons. Cook, stirring frequently, until of the consistency of honey, and seal in half-pint jars, as for canned fruit.

Fruit Leathers by Deanna F. Darling

If after making all these jellies, jams, preserves, conserves, marmalades, butters and honeys, you still have on hand lots of pears, peaches, apricots, plums, grapes or strawberries, for example, there is yet another way to preserve these perishable fruits for winter enjoyment — make fruit leather.

To prepare the leather, wash fruit well and pit. If using substandard specimens, cut out bad spots on skin. Drop fruits into the blender a few halves at a time with the dial set at purée. Continue until you have about three cups.

If using very ripe apricots, no sweetening is needed. If the fruit is very tart add honey as desired, starting with 1 tablespoon and increasing only as necessary; 1/2 teaspoon of cinnamon blended with 3 cups of purée adds taste variety. Peaches and pears need no sweetening; however, you can add 1 tablespoon of lemon juice and 1/2 teaspoon of cinnamon for every 3 cups if variety is desired.

Wild strawberry leather makes delicious nibbling and can be melted for a glaze to use on tarts or a ham. Use 2 pounds of strawberries, hulled, and 1/2 cup honey. Add some powdered sugar. In a saucepan, simmer the berries and honey over low heat, stirring and mashing the fruit as it cooks until it is as thick as you can get it. Spread on a flat dish and place in the sun to dry. Sprinkle with powdered sugar, cut into squares and store in glass jars. Or, roll it like a jelly roll, then slice and store in glass jars.

To produce a paper-thin leather, lightly oil a cookie sheet, or cover it with a layer of foil or waxed food wrap. Spread purée 1/4-inch thick, smoothing with a spoon, if necessary, to cover evenly. Place in a 120°F to 150°F oven, leaving the door slightly ajar for steam to escape. Two cookie sheets can be put in the oven at the same time to utilize oven heat more efficiently.

If you prefer not to use the oven, spread the fruit blend on cookie sheets and dry outdoors in the sun. The amount of time it will take to dry will depend on the thickness of the purée and the outdoor temperature. If the sun is hot (and the temperature 80°F or more), drying will take approximately eight to ten hours. If the weather is cool and the purée quite thick, it may take a week or two. Do not leave the purée outdoors overnight.

When making large amounts of fruit in very hot weather, you might prefer to spread a sheet of plastic wrap directly on a large table top and pour a thin layer of purée over it. Keep the table in the sun at all times. If you wish to cover the leather with a net for insect protection, do so, but delay placing the net for the first hour or two because it will stick to the fresh fruit blend.

When the leather has hardened, ease the edge up. Peel off easily. Roll into a scroll, or into jelly-roll shape and place in a cloth or paper bag to continue drying for several days. The finished product, which should still be pliable like leather, can be stored in tightly closed glass jars, but make sure the rolls are completely dry. If they are not, the leather will mold. If the leather has dried to the brittle stage, you can soften it by placing a piece of apple in the jar for two or three days. This will give it some moisture.

If you find yourself with so much fruit that you can't locate sufficient space to dry it before it spoils, freeze the purée for drying later. When ready to do up a batch of leather, partially thaw and purée the fruit, and proceed as previously explained. Don't fret if the fruit discolors slightly; it will darken as it dries anyway.

Fruit leather is ideal for snacking, a welcome addition to any lunch, and the perfect traveling companion.